The leaders of the Mongols said
to the young Genghis Khan:
We will make you khan....
And if we disobey your command,
separate us from our families,
from our ladies and wives.
Separate us, and throw down
our heads upon the ground!
If we disobey you, exile us
and throw us out into the wilderness.

Excerpt from **The History of the Life of Genghis Khan: The Secret History of the Mongols**

In memory of F.W. Mote

Photographs © 2008: akg-Images, London: 36, 84 top (Bibliothèque Nationale de France/VISIOARS), 86 bottom, 112 (British Library, London), 102 (Werner Forman), 10 (National Palace Museum, Taipei), 82 left; Art Resource, NY: 74 (Bibliothèque Nationale, Paris, France), 32, 64, 83 top, 85 top (Bildarchiv Preussischer Kulturbesitz), 84 bottom (Victoria & Albert Museum, London); Bibliothèque Nationale de France: 44, 56, 83 bottom; Bridgeman Art Library International Ltd., London/New York: 67, 85 bottom, 93 (Bibliothèque Nationale, Paris, France), 86 top (British Museum, London, UK), 52 (Alphonse Hubrecht/ Private Collection), 71 (Private Collection); Corbis Images: 87 bottom (Dean Conger), 78, 79 (Michel Setboun); Getty Images: 34 (Hulton Archive), 82 right (Bruno Morandi), 60 (MPI), 22 (Gordon Wiltsie); Courtesy of John Man: 19; Mary Evans Picture Library: 117; Michel Setboun: 26; North Wind Picture Archives: 47; Peter Arnold Inc./Hartmut Schwarzbach: 41; Superstock, Inc./age fotostock: 104; The Art Archive/Picture Desk/British Library, London: 87 top; The Granger Collection, New York: 97, 109.

Illustrations by XNR Productions, Inc.: 4, 5, 8, 9
Cover art, page 8 inset by Mark Summers
Chapter art by Roland Sarkany

Library of Congress Cataloging-in-Publication Data

Goldberg, Enid A.
Genghis Khan : 13th-century Mongolian tyrant / Enid A. Goldberg and Norman Itzkowitz.
p. cm. – (A wicked history)
Includes bibliographical references and index.
ISBN-13: 978-0-531-12596-0 (lib. bdg.) 978-0-531-13895-3 (pbk.)
ISBN-10: 0-531-12596-3 (lib. bdg.) 0-531-13895-X (pbk.)
1. Genghis Khan, 1162-1227. 2. Mongols—Kings and rulers—Biography.
I. Itzkowitz, Norman. II. Title.
DS22.G45G65 2007
950'.21092—dc22
[B]
2007008711

Tod Olson, Series Editor
Marie O'Neill, Art Director
Allicette Torres, Cover Design
SimonSays Design!, Book Design and Production

14 15 R 17 16 15 23

A WICKED HISTORY™

Genghis Khan

13th-CENTURY MONGOLIAN TYRANT

ENID A. GOLDBERG &
NORMAN ITZKOWITZ

Franklin Watts
An Imprint of Scholastic Inc.
New York Toronto London Auckland Sydney
Mexico City New Delhi Hong Kong
Danbury, Connecticut

The Mongolian Empire

Genghis Khan unified the tribes of the Mongolian steppe and then built an empire.

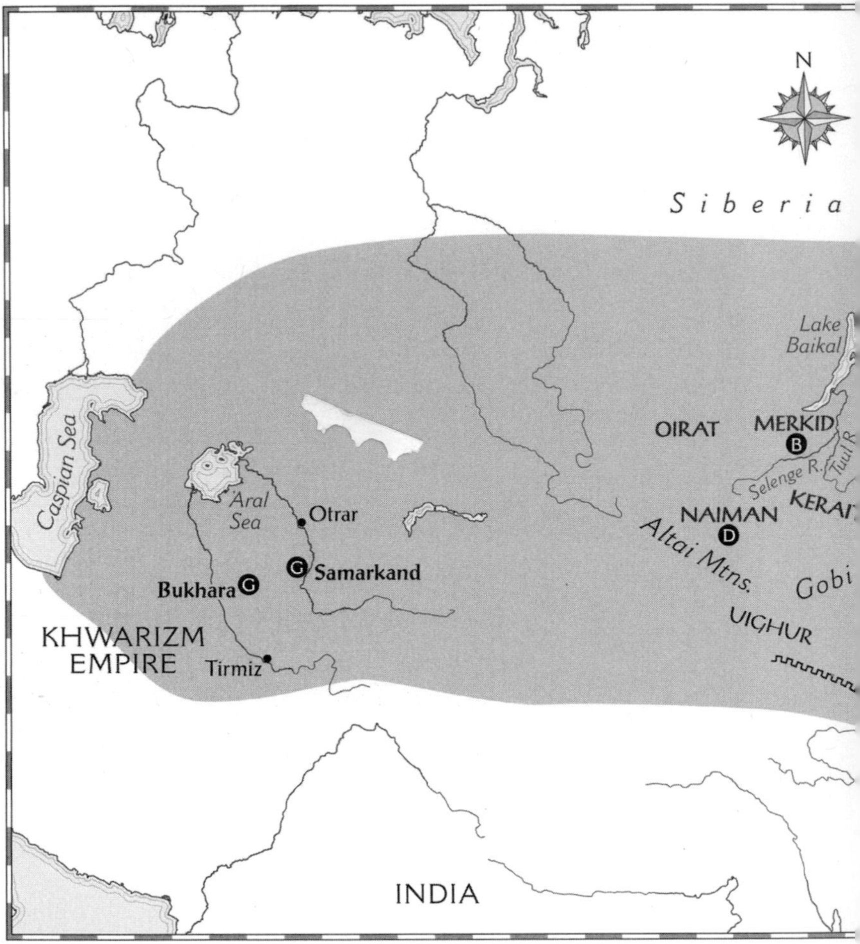

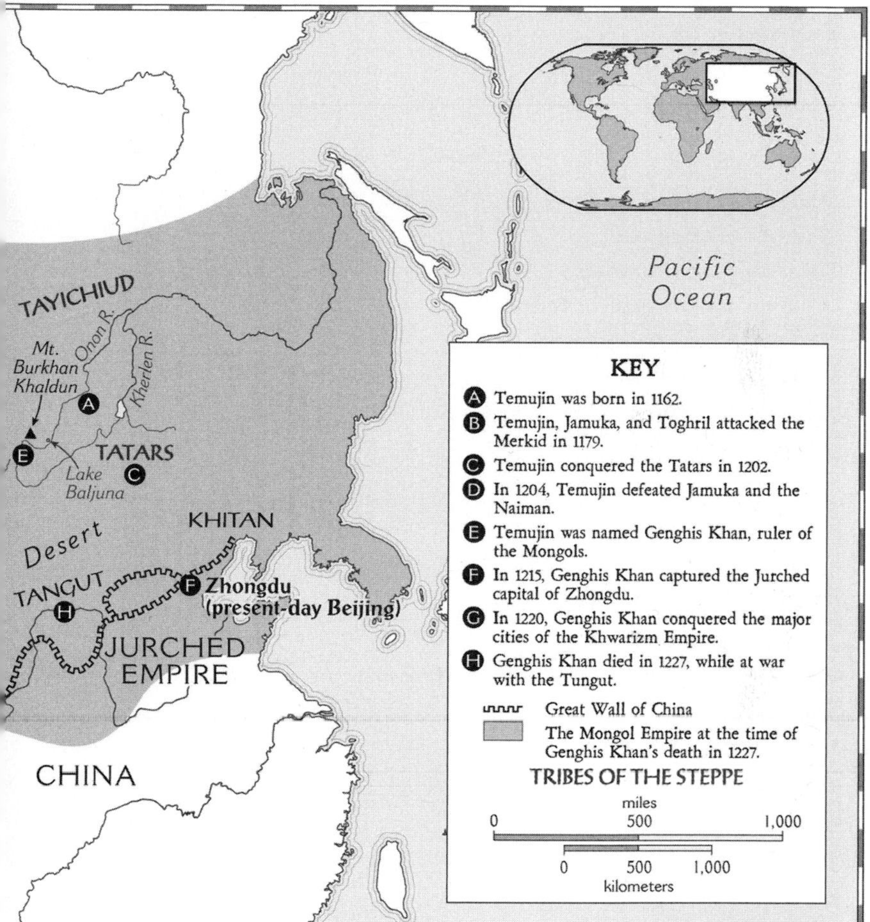
Pacific
Ocean
TAYICHIUD
Onon R.
Kherlen R.
Mt.
Burkhan
Khaldun
TATARS
Lake
Baljuna
Desert
KHITAN
TANGUT
Zhongdu
(present-day Beijing)
JURCHED
EMPIRE
CHINA
KEY
A Temujin was born in 1162.
B Temujin, Jamuka, and Toghril attacked the Merkid in 1179.
C Temujin conquered the Tatars in 1202.
D In 1204, Temujin defeated Jamuka and the Naiman.
E Temujin was named Genghis Khan, ruler of the Mongols.
F In 1215, Genghis Khan captured the Jurched capital of Zhongdu.
G In 1220, Genghis Khan conquered the major cities of the Khwarizm Empire.
H Genghis Khan died in 1227, while at war with the Tungut.
Great Wall of China
The Mongol Empire at the time of Genghis Khan's death in 1227.
TRIBES OF THE STEPPE
miles
0
500
1,000
0
500
1,000
kilometers

Table of Contents

A Wicked Web

A look at the allies and enemies of Genghis Khan.

Family and Friends

YESUGEI
Genghis Khan's father

HOELUN
his mother

BEGTER
a half brother

BELGUTEI
a half brother

KHASAR
a brother

BORTE
his first wife

JOCHI, CHAGATAI, OGODEI, AND TOLUI
his sons

GENGHIS KHAN

BOORCHU, JELME, MUKALI, AND JEBE
trusted advisors and military commanders

JAMUKA
his childhood friend

TOGHRIL
leader of the Kerait, one of Genghis Khan's early allies, and later his rival

Tribes of the Steppe

THE MONGOLS
Temujin's people, a loose collection of tribes and clans (family groups); they were nomads and lived in the northeastern part of what is today Mongolia

THE JURKIN
a clan related to Temujin's clan

THE TAYICHIUD
one of the most powerful Mongol clans

To the East

THE TATARS
longtime enemies of the Mongols; by trading with the Jurched to the south, they became the richest of the steppe tribes

To the west

THE KERAIT
a Christian tribe that traded with the wealthy cities of Central Asia; their leader was **Toghril**

THE MERKID
a warlike tribe whose warriors rode tamed reindeer; Genghis Khan's mother was stolen from the Merkid

THE NAIMAN
a powerful tribe with strong ties to the Muslim people of Central Asia

THE OIRAT
a forest tribe closely related to the Merkid

Beyond the Steppe

THE JURCHED
a wealthy empire in what is now northern China; their ruler was known as the **Golden Khan**

THE KHITAN
a tribe that the Jurched had conquered in northern China; they became Genghis Khan's allies against the Jurched

KHWARIZM
Muslim empire to the west of the Mongols, in Central Asia; it was ruled by **Sultan Muhammad II**

THE TANGUT AND THE UIGHUR
tribes to the south of the Mongols, beyond the Gobi desert

GENGHIS KHAN, c. 1162–1227

Tirmiz, Central Asia, 1220

IN THE YEAR 1220, A WAVE OF TERROR SWEPT ACROSS CENTRAL ASIA. More than 100,000 Mongol warriors rode west across the dry plains. They wore wool robes and fur hats. On their backs they carried bows and razor-sharp arrows.

They were an army like no one had seen before. They traveled light and moved fast. They fought with great discipline. Each soldier obeyed his commander with fierce loyalty. Each commander took orders from the leader of all the Mongols, Genghis Khan.

Their goal was to conquer the known world.

That summer, the Mongols arrived at the walled city of Tirmiz. The thunder of horses' hooves shook the ground around the Oxus River. A cloud of dust darkened the sky. Mongol horsemen surrounded the city. Genghis Khan sent a warrior inside with a simple message: Surrender or be killed.

Inside the walls, the people of Tirmiz had heard the rumors. The Mongols destroyed farmland as they rode. They burnt crops and ruined watering systems. They attacked powerful cities. In the spring, they had captured Bukhara and Samarkand. Bukhara was burned to the ground. The conquering warriors supposedly killed tens of thousands of people. They made slaves of thousands more.

Tirmiz, however, refused to surrender. For ten days, the city's soldiers battled the Mongols. They shot arrows at the horsemen. They used catapults to launch stones.

On the eleventh day, the Mongols silenced the defenders. They stormed into the city. All the people, men and women, were driven outside the walls. The prisoners were divided among the warriors and killed.

Finally, the slaughter stopped. According to one story, a single woman survived. She offered the Mongols a large pearl in exchange for her life. The warriors asked to see the pearl. But the woman said she had swallowed it. In response, the Mongols ripped open her stomach. Inside, they found several pearls.

When Genghis Khan was shown the pearls, he gave an order. He sent his warriors to search for more pearls in the fields of the dead. One by one they ripped open the stomachs of the people they had killed.

It's a gruesome story. Many more like it have been told about Genghis Khan. Some were invented by his enemies. Some were told by the Mongols themselves to make their enemies fear them. Plenty more were absolutely true. Genghis Khan did not need lies to prove his ruthlessness. The story of his life is enough.

Part 1

Temujin of the Mongolian Steppe

CHAPTER 1

Born on the Steppe

Genghis Khan's life started with AN ACT OF VIOLENCE.

IN HIS LIFETIME, Genghis Khan conquered lands that stretched for 3,000 miles. He was *khan*—or leader—of millions of people. He was the most feared man in the world. Yet for centuries his life was a mystery.

No one knew what the great khan looked like. He never allowed anyone to paint his portrait.

No one knew where he was buried. According to one story, 800 horsemen rode over his grave to hide any sign of it. The horsemen were then killed by soldiers so they couldn't reveal the secret. The entire area was closed to outsiders for centuries.

Who was this great warrior? Historians had old records of the battles he won and the cities he burned. But they didn't know where he was born, how he grew up, or what he was like. There were rumors of a secret book, written just after he died. But his descendants kept it locked away. Over the years, people assumed it had been lost forever.

Then, in the 1880s, a copy of *The Secret History of the Mongols* was found in China. It took about 100 years for it to be translated into English. Finally, the story of Genghis Khan could be told.

According to *The Secret History*, the story begins with an act of violence.

The year was probably 1161. Small bands of hunters and herders traveled the steppe—grasslands in the area today known as Mongolia. One day, the man who would become Genghis Khan's father was hunting with his falcon near the Onon River. He was the leader of a small group of Mongols belonging to the Tayichiud clan. His name was Yesugei.

In the distance, Yesugei saw a cart carrying a young woman and her new husband. He rode close enough to spy on the two travelers. The woman was beautiful. Yesugei wanted her for his wife. He rode off to get help from his two brothers.

The brothers rode hard until the cart came into view. The husband was a Merkid tribesman named Chiledu. His wife belonged to a tribe from the eastern steppe. When the brothers charged, Chiledu fled for his life. Yesugei rode up and told the woman that she had a new husband.

The woman was furious. But in the lawless world of the Mongolian steppe, she had no choice. She told her captors that her name was Hoelun. Then she followed Yesugei to her new home.

The following year, Yesugei rode off to attack a clan from the nearby Tatar tribe. He returned to find that Hoelun had given birth to a baby boy. Yesugei

YESUGEI AND HIS BROTHERS close in
on the cart carrying Hoelun.

named his son Temujin, after a Tatar prisoner he had captured. Yesugei may have hoped that his military success would bring his son luck. He could not have known that Temujin would become the most successful warrior of his time.

Mongolia in Temujin's Time

TEMUJIN GREW UP ON THE MONGOLIAN STEPPE. Flat, dry grassland stretched as far as the eye could see. Far to the east and west, mountains rose 10,000 feet off the plains. To the south lay the vast Gobi desert.

Like most people on the steppe, Temujin lived in an extended family, or clan. These clans were nomadic. They followed the seasons from campsite to campsite. They survived by hunting or herding sheep and goats. They lived in round felt tents called *yurts*.

Many clans were part of a larger tribe. In Temujin's time several tribes controlled the steppe. Temujin's clan belonged to the Mongols. To the west were the Merkid, the Kerait, the Oirat, and the powerful Naiman. To the east lay the Tatars.

The tribes of the steppe were divided and poor. They traded for clothes and metal goods with wealthier nations. They also raided each other for loot.

This weak collection of tribes was young Temujin's world. Turn to the map on pages 4–5 to see how he turned it into the most powerful nation on earth.

CHAPTER 2

Abandoned

Temujin gains a fiancée and LOSES NEARLY EVERYTHING ELSE.

TEMUJIN GREW UP along the Onon River. He played with his brothers and other children. Early in life, they learned to ride horses. By age four, most Mongolian children rode alone without saddles. They shot arrows at targets made from small leather pouches. They even learned to ride standing up. They often had contests to see who could knock the other off his horse.

HORSES WERE A PRIZED POSSESSION on the steppe. Like these Mongolian boys, Temujin learned to ride at an early age.

In the winter, the boys played on the frozen river. Each child carried a set of dice-like toys called knucklebones. Knucklebones were made from the anklebones of sheep. They could be used to settle arguments, to predict the future, or to play games.

On the steppe, kids grew up fast. When Temujin was nine years old, his father decided to find him a bride. Father and son saddled their horses and rode off. Yesugei hoped to find Temujin a wife from his mother's clan. But before they found Hoelun's family, they stopped to visit a man named Dei the Wise. Dei was impressed with Temujin. The boy "had fire in his eyes and light in his face," he said.

Dei boasted that the women of his clan were known for their beauty. He introduced Yesugei to his daughter Borte. The girl was lively, and as beautiful as her father had claimed. She was just a year older than Temujin.

Both men agreed that their children would marry. Temujin stayed on to live and work for Dei's family until the wedding. Yesugei left for home.

Some weeks later, a messenger arrived in Dei's camp with bad news. On his way home, Yesugei had stopped to eat with a Tatar clan. The clan recognized him as an enemy. They slipped poison into Yesugei's food. Temujin's father limped home, where he now lay dying.

Temujin rode home as fast as possible, but it was too late. His father was dead. And Temujin's life was about to change forever.

Without Yesugei, Temujin's mother had no status in the clan. Family ties were important to the Mongols. And since Hoelun did not come from Yesugei's clan, people began to ignore her. They refused to share food. Eventually, the clan's new leaders gave the order to leave Hoelun's family behind.

One day, Temujin woke at dawn. The clan members were loading their carts and moving on. An older man spoke up for Temujin's family. The clan had no right to leave the family behind, he yelled. A chief turned and drove a spear through the man's body. The clan rode off, leaving the man to die.

Temujin was just nine years old. His family was left to scrape out a living on the dry steppe by themselves.

CHAPTER 3

Blood Brothers

Temujin makes a friend for life—OR SO HE THINKS.

LEFT ALONE, HOELUN TOOK CHARGE of her family. She had five boys to support. Three of them were her children. The other two were Temujin's half brothers. Their mother was Yesugei's first wife. They too had been left behind by the clan.

Everyone went to work finding food. Hoelun gathered fruits and berries. She dug up plant roots to cook and eat. The older boys made arrows from animal bones. They turned their mother's sewing needles into fishhooks. The whole family hunted

TEMUJIN THREW KNUCKLEBONES for fun when he was growing up. More than 800 years later, Mongolians still play this game.

and fished. They caught dogs and mice and other small animals. They ate the meat and used the skins to make clothing.

The family sometimes shared campsites with people from other clans. Over time, Temujin made friends and allies. One of these friends stood out above all the others. His name was Jamuka.

Jamuka's family camped during the winter near Temujin's family. The boys hunted and played together. They threw knucklebones. Perhaps they raced on horseback. They grew as close as brothers.

At age 11 or 12, Temujin and Jamuka became *andas*, or blood brothers. They gave each other arrowheads. Jamuka made a special arrow for Temujin. It whistled as it flew threw the air. They probably held a special ceremony. In Mongol culture *andas* promised their friendship by drinking each other's blood. In this way, their bond became stronger than the bond between true brothers.

The next winter, Jamuka's family did not return. The two friends drifted apart. They would meet again as warriors. And at least for a time, the two childhood friends would make strong allies.

Chapter 4

Blood Between Brothers

A family rivalry TURNS DEADLY.

TEMUJIN MADE ENEMIES as easily as he made friends. His half brother, Begter, became the first.

With their father gone, the boys fought for leadership of the family. As the oldest, Begter had the strongest claim. He seemed determined to put Temujin in his place. One day, Temujin shot a bird and Begter stole it. On another day, Temujin and his full brother Khasar went fishing. Begter and their other half brother, Belgutei, joined them. This time, Begter stole a fish from Temujin.

Temujin went straight to his mother to complain. Hoelun scolded Temujin. The family had to stick together, she said. They had no one else to rely on but each other.

Temujin left in anger. He and Khasar decided they would have to act alone. They were barely in their teens. Yet they decided to kill their half brother.

Temujin planned the murder. He and Khasar stalked their half brother. They found him sitting alone, watching the family's horses. Temujin sneaked up behind Begter. He sent Khasar around to the front. The brothers raised their bows.

Begter made no move to escape. He simply asked Temujin to let Belgutei live. Temujin agreed. Then he and Khasar drove their arrows into Begter's body. They left their half brother to bleed to death in the grass.

The two boys returned to the yurt. Hoelun exploded in anger when she found out about the cold-blooded murder. Her sons were like wild dogs, like panthers, like monsters, she said. "Now you have no companion other than your shadow."

Temujin, however, did have Khasar. He had Jamuka, wherever he was. And he stood alone as the leader of his family. Temujin had proven two things at a very young age: He could be loyal to his friends—and absolutely ruthless with his enemies.

CHAPTER 5

Capture and Escape

TEMUJIN IS SAVED by his own courage and the kindness of strangers.

NOT LONG AFTER BEGTER'S DEATH, Temujin was forced to defend his new-found power. A group of warriors from the Tayichiud clan arrived outside his camp. The Tayichiud were the strongest clan in the area. Their people had deserted Hoelun after Yesugei's death. Now they were back. And the warriors made it clear that they were looking for Temujin.

MONGOL WARRIORS OFTEN TOOK PRISONERS
in raids on other tribes. Temujin was held in a wooden yoke like the ones shown here.

Temujin's family held them off while Temujin fled into the forest. He hid in the trees for nine days. Finally, he stumbled out, starving and tired. The Tayichiud warriors were waiting for him.

Temujin became a prisoner in the Tayichiud camp. His captors locked his neck in a wooden yoke. They made servant families watch over him. Each night they moved him to a different tent.

Temujin waited for the right moment to escape. He chose the night of a big festival. His guards were drinking heavily. They left a young boy in charge of the prisoner. When Temujin was alone with the boy, he swung the yoke. He knocked his young guard down with a blow to the head. Then he ran for safety.

Before long, the forest was crawling with Tayichiud. Temujin hid in the tall weeds near a riverbank. An old man discovered him, and Temujin got ready to run. But the old man made no move to capture him.

Temujin recognized the man from one of his nights as a prisoner. The old man's family members were servants of the Tayichiud. On the night Temujin stayed with them, they had been kind to him. Maybe they would help him now, he thought.

After dark, Temujin found his way to the old man's tent. The family helped him take the yoke off. Then they hid him in a cart full of wool. The next night, they gave him some food and a horse. Free at last, Temujin rode off to rejoin his family.

TEMUJIN HID in a cart of wool while the Tayichiud warriors searched for him.

Temujin had survived his first clash with another clan. He was still just a teenager. But he had planned his escape with intelligence and courage. And ordinary people seemed to be drawn to him. Temujin was beginning to look like a leader.

CHAPTER 6

Allies

TEMUJIN FINDS A WIFE and a new father.

AT 16, TEMUJIN DECIDED it was time to marry. He set out with Belgutei to find Borte. She was 17 by now, almost too old to get married. But she was still waiting for Temujin.

Borte's family was thrilled to see the boy they had liked so much seven years earlier. He was nearly a man now. They were happy to honor their promise. And they gave him a valuable coat made of sable fur as a marriage gift.

Temujin rode proudly home with his new bride.

TOGHRIL, LEADER OF THE KERAIT, supposedly lived in a golden yurt like this one. This illustration was drawn for a book by a Persian historian in the 1300s.

Finally, he was not alone. He had companionship. But Borte brought him more than that. Her clan stood ready to support Temujin's family in any way. For the first time since his father died, Temujin had real allies.

Now, it was time to reach out again. Temujin looked to the Kerait tribe, who lived just to the west. They were wealthier than the Mongols. The Kerait were Christians. They traded with the wealthy cities of Central Asia. Their leader was a man named Toghril. He supposedly lived in a golden yurt. His household drank from golden goblets. To marry a Kerait princess, a man had to offer 200 servants as a gift.

Toghril was a risky choice for an ally. He had killed his brothers in order to take control of the tribe. But Temujin was ready to trust him. Toghril and Temujin's father had once been *andas*, like Temujin and Jamuka. The Kerait leader's friendship would help protect Temujin and his family.

Temujin left his new bride at home. He saddled up with Khasar and Belgutei. Together they went to visit Toghril. When they arrived, Temujin handed Toghril the sable coat. He reminded the Kerait leader of his friendship with Yesugei. "You are as my own father," he said.

Toghril accepted the gift with pleasure. Young Temujin had a powerful ally on the steppe.

CHAPTER 7

Kidnapped!

BORTE IS STOLEN. Will Temujin go to war to win her back?

WHILE TEMUJIN WAS GAINING ALLIES, he also added friends to his camp. A young man named Boorchu joined the tiny group. A year or two earlier, Boorchu had helped Temujin recover some stolen horses. A boy named Jelme also moved in. He became Temujin's servant. Jelme's father had long ago promised his son to Temujin's father.

Despite Temujin's growing power, his band was still small. And they had plenty of enemies. One tribe, in particular, carried an old grudge: the Merkid.

Early one morning, Hoelun's servant awoke with a start. Lying with her ear to the ground, she heard the sound of horses' hooves. She felt the earth tremble. Were the terrible Tayichiud back again?

The servant's screams woke Hoelun. Soon everyone was awake. The men scrambled for their horses. So did Hoelun, carrying Temujin's little sister in her lap. Only Borte did not have a horse.

The horsemen were closing in fast. Temujin had to act quickly. He ordered his mother's servant to stay behind. He and the others rode off to hide in the forests of Mount Burkhan Khaldun. Borte and the old woman were left to the attackers.

Soon after the men had gone, several warriors rode into camp. They were Merkid tribesman. Some 17 years before, Yesugei had stolen Hoelun from their relative, Chiledu. Chiledu was now dead, but his clan had not forgotten Yesugei's crime.

The Merkid found Borte hidden in a cart full of wool. The warriors took her prisoner. As they rode off, they turned and shouted, "We have our revenge."

When the Merkid had gone, Temujin came out of hiding. His wife was gone. But once again, he had been saved. The Mongol gods, it seemed, were protecting him. He offered a prayer to Burkhan Khaldun, which means "God Mountain." He knelt and prayed to the sun. He sprinkled milk on the ground to thank the spirits of the earth.

Now, Temujin had a decision to make. Three rivers flowed from Burkhan Khaldun. The Kherlen River led to the steppe. There was pasture land there. He could keep horses and sheep. Yet he would not be able to protect himself from the Merkid or the Tayichiud. The Onon River led to more wooded land. It offered protection. But he would have to scrape out a living the way he did as a child.

The third river, the Tuul, led toward the Kerait and his new ally, Toghril. Toghril could help Temujin find Borte. He could put together an army to attack the Merkid. It was Temujin's only chance to free Borte. But he would have to go to war to do it.

After three days of prayer, Temujin left with Khasar and Belgutei. They followed the Tuul southwest to find Toghril.

THE TUUL RIVER FLOWS SOUTHWEST from Burkhan Khaldun. Temujin followed it to the land of his new ally, Toghril.

CHAPTER 8

First Blood

With the help of an old friend, TEMUJIN GOES TO WAR.

TOGHRIL AGREED IMMEDIATELY to help Temujin. *The Secret History* says he promised 20,000 warriors to attack the Merkid. He would get 20,000 more from another ally. That ally was Temujin's long-lost *anda*, Jamuka.

Temujin hadn't seen Jamuka in several years. He sent a message to his old friend. He told him about Borte's kidnapping. The Merkid had taken his wife, Temujin said. They had broken his heart. He needed Jamuka's help to make his heart whole again.

Jamuka answered right away. His old friend's story made him sad, he said. Like Temujin, Jamuka had been through hard times. And he, too, hated the Merkid. Years earlier, he had been attacked and robbed by a Merkid chief. Now, he was once again strong. He was ready to go to war. "I have grasped my steel-tipped spear," he said. "I have set my peach-bark arrow in the bow. Let us go on horseback and strike the Merkid."

The forces joined up and marched north into Merkid territory. They built rafts to cross rivers. Yet they barely had to raise their weapons. A Merkid hunting party saw the attackers coming. The hunters rushed back to their camps. As Jamuka and Temujin rode in along the Selenge River, the Merkid were already fleeing.

Temujin raced from yurt to yurt, yelling for Borte. But Borte had no idea who the attackers were. She had been given as a wife to Chiledu's brother. When her new husband ran, she ran with him.

Suddenly, Borte heard Temujin's voice in the darkness. She broke away and ran toward the sound.

Temujin rode, shouting her name again and again. When she finally caught up to him, he didn't recognize her in the night. Thinking Borte was a Merkid, he nearly attacked her. When he saw who it was, he took her into his arms. "I have found what I came for," he said.

Temujin asked Toghril and Jamuka to call off the attack. The Mongols took everything they could find in the Merkid camps. But Temujin felt no need to chase the Merkid. He had won his first battle. He was wealthy with loot. He had his wife and his *anda* back. Temujin had exactly what he wanted—at least for now.

BORTE RETURNED TO TEMUJIN'S CAMP after spending months as a prisoner of the Merkid.

CHAPTER 9

Friends for Life?

Can Jamuka and Temujin KEEP THEIR VOW?

AFTER THE BATTLE, Temujin joined with Jamuka's tribe. The old friends rode ahead alone. Once again, they declared themselves to be blood brothers. This time, they held a public ceremony. They exchanged gifts from the Merkid loot. They gave each other golden sashes and fine horses. They feasted and danced and drank. Then, like brothers, they spent the night under the same blanket.

Jamuka and Temujin spent the next year and a half together. During this time, Temujin's following grew.

Borte gave birth to a son. The boy's father may have been a Merkid. But Temujin named him Jochi and treated him as his own. Temujin also had loot to give away. Gifts bought him loyalty from the people of the steppe.

Still, there was no question that Jamuka was the leader of the band. He was the one who had raised an army of thousands. Most of the tribal leaders in the area supported him. While Temujin stayed with Jamuka, he would always be a follower.

In the summer of 1181, the friendship fell apart. Jamuka stopped treating Temujin as an equal. One day, he ordered Temujin to camp in a separate area with the sheep and goats. Temujin felt insulted. But had he misunderstood Jamuka? Temujin went to ask his mother for advice. Borte was there, too, and she interrupted the conversation. Jamuka had gotten tired of them, she said. It was time to leave.

That night, Jamuka stopped to set up camp. Temujin and his small band quietly kept going. Many of Jamuka's followers went with him.

As he crossed the steppe, Temujin must have felt the excitement of the moment. After so many years alone, he now had a tribe of his own. He was just 19, yet people looked to him as a leader. The future was full of possibility.

Over the next 25 years, Temujin and his blood brother would become fierce rivals. They would steal horses and women from each other. Their armies would battle on the steppe. In the end, only one of them would be left to rule over all the Mongol tribes.

TEMUJIN LEFT HIS BLOOD BROTHER and rode across the steppe. For the first time in his life, he had his own followers.

PART 2/

Khan of the Mongols

CHAPTER 10

A Bid for Power

Temujin gains strength and prepares FOR BATTLE WITH JAMUKA.

WITHIN A FEW YEARS, one thing was clear. The steppe had two strong leaders: Jamuka and Temujin. Both men had gained followers. And both of them seemed to have the same goal in mind: They wanted to bring the divided Mongol tribes together under a single khan. It was time for the clans of the steppe to choose sides.

Little by little, Temujin gained power. He used his wealth wisely. He gave horses and furs to his followers. He helped poor clans hunt for food. For many years, the

Tayichiud—the clan that had captured Temujin when he was a young man—had been the strongest in the area. And they had terrorized the weaker clans. To many people, Temujin seemed like a better alternative.

Mongol shamans, or priests, began to say that the gods favored Temujin. A man named Korchi arrived from Jamuka's camp. He said he had seen a talking ox. "Heaven and Earth have agreed that Temujin shall be Lord of the Empire," the ox said. A shaman named Teb-tengri also came to join Temujin. He claimed that God had spoken to him. God said, "I have given the whole surface of the earth to Temujin and to his sons."

As Temujin's power grew, his allies decided to name him khan. Temujin was still in his twenties at the time. The clans gathered at a camp along the Kimurka Stream.

Temujin's followers promised their loyalty to the new khan. They pledged to hunt animals for Temujin. They would lead men into battle for him. After victory, they would bring back beautiful women, tents, and horses. They gave Temujin the right to punish them if they disobeyed his orders. "Separate us . . . from our wives and women and throw our heads away on the empty steppe," they said.

The words were impressive. But so far they were just words. Temujin was khan in name only. Most of the tribal leaders still supported Jamuka. Temujin had to turn his followers into a force that would bring all the Mongols into his camp.

A SHAMAN PREDICTS THE FUTURE, as Temujin (top) looks on. Mongol nomads often took advice from spiritual leaders.

CHAPTER 11

Brotherly War

TEMUJIN BEGINS TO BUILD A NATION—and tries to defend it.

TEMUJIN HAD COME A LONG WAY. He began with just his family and his friends, Boorchu and Jelme. As a boy, he ate roots, berries, and mouse meat. His family had just nine horses. They lived in fear of losing all they owned to robbers.

Now, Temujin had the beginnings of a nation. He began to bring order to the wandering Mongol clans. In most tribes, the leader's family members held the important positions. But Temujin valued loyalty and talent above everything else. Boorchu and Jelme were not relatives. But they had earned Temujin's trust. They became his closest advisors.

Safety was another important goal. Temujin named 150 warriors to guard the camp day and night. Khasar, the best archer in camp, took charge of the guards. Belgutei took care of the tribe's best horses. They were kept close to camp in case they were needed quickly. Some of Temujin's most trusted friends became cooks. Yesugei, after all, had been poisoned. Temujin did not want his life to end the same way.

As he organized his people, Temujin spread the news of his election as khan. He sent a message to Toghril. Temujin claimed that he had no desire to become more powerful than the Kerait leader. He simply wanted to unite the tribes of the steppe under Toghril's leadership.

Toghril sent his blessing. Jamuka's growing power was beginning to worry the Kerait leader. He must have hoped that Temujin's strength would keep Jamuka occupied.

For his part, Jamuka was not pleased to hear the news. There is an old Mongol saying, *You cannot have two bears in one cave.* Jamuka, who also wanted to be khan of all the Mongols, felt the cave belonged to him.

The two bears, Jamuka and Temujin, were headed for battle. All they needed was an excuse to fight.

The excuse came from a common event on the steppe. One of Jamuka's men stole some horses from a tribesman who was loyal to Temujin. The tribesman chased the thief and killed him.

Jamuka set out to take revenge. He put together an army and attacked Temujin. Outnumbered, Temujin suffered a devastating defeat. Once again, he ran for the mountain. He led his remaining warriors up the Onon River valley. They hid in a narrow pass, high in the mountain.

Jamuka decided not to chase Temujin. Instead, he rode back to his camp. There, he took out his anger on Temujin's followers. According to one story, he boiled 70 prisoners to death. To the Mongols, boiling

JAMUKA SUPPOSEDLY HAD SOME MONGOL PRISONERS boiled alive. This picture shows the feet of some victims who suffered this horrible punishment.

was a dishonorable way to kill your enemy. It killed the soul as well as the body. Another account says that Jamuka chopped off the heads of two princes. He tied the heads to the tail of his horse. Then he rode off across the steppe.

Whatever Jamuka actually did, he may have gone too far. He defeated his rival. He made his enemies fear him. But he also horrified his allies.

It would take time for Temujin to recover from the defeat. But he would come back stronger than ever.

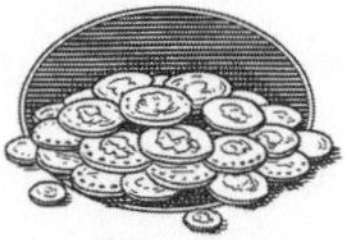

CHAPTER 12

Attacking the Tatars

Temujin takes on an old enemy—AND DESTROYS A NEW ONE.

TEMUJIN WORKED HARD to rebuild his tribe. Jamuka's cruelty after their battle seemed to help him. According to *The Secret History*, several clans deserted Jamuka and joined up with Temujin.

Then, in 1195, Temujin got a new opportunity. It came from the Jurched, who lived in what is now China. The Jurched were far wealthier than the Mongols. Their ruler was known as the

Golden Khan. He lived in a huge palace in Zhongdu (today's Beijing). The Golden Khan and his princes slept on silk pillows and blankets. They wore beautiful jewelry made from gold, silver, and ivory. They made furniture from special woods, and bowls from fine porcelain.

Yesugei's old enemies, the Tatars, acted as policemen for the Jurched. They made sure that no Mongol tribe became strong enough to threaten the Golden Khan. They also controlled the flow of treasures to the Mongols.

But in 1195, a Tatar prince got a little too powerful. He rebelled against the Jurched. The Jurched attacked the rebellious prince and called on Toghril for help. Toghril asked Temujin to join him in battle.

Temujin had good reasons to go to war. His father had been poisoned by Tatars 25 years earlier. On the steppe, it was never too late to take revenge. Temujin also needed the loot and the fame that a victory would bring.

That victory came easily. Temujin and Toghril routed the rebel Tatars and killed their chief. The Mongols rode away with plenty of loot. Temujin took a silver cradle belonging to the chief. He also took a quilt decorated with pearls. Even the captured children had treasures to offer. Some of them wore satin clothes and gold jewelry.

The Tatar battle gave Temujin new life. He returned home with his troops. And in 1197, he threw them back into battle. This time, he took on the Jurkin tribe. The Jurkin were distant relatives of Temujin's clan. They had promised their help against the Tatars. But they hadn't shown up when Temujin gathered his troops. What's more, they had raided Temujin's base camp while he was battling the Tatars.

The Jurkin didn't stand a chance against Temujin's warriors. Temujin defeated them and took many prisoners. Then he prepared to send a message to the people of the steppe.

Temujin called his followers together. He held

NO MERCY: Temujin (upper right) looks on while a prisoner is whipped.

a public trial for the Jurkin leaders. Temujin found his relatives guilty. Killing tribal leaders who were related to your own clan was a crime among the Mongols. Temujin ignored the rule completely. He had the Jurkin leaders' heads chopped off, one by one. Their bodies were thrown onto the steppe without a proper burial.

Temujin dealt with the common people in a different way. Often, the Mongols made slaves of their prisoners. Instead, Temujin made the Jurkin people part of his own tribe. As long as they were loyal, they would remain free. He even gave his mother a Jurkin child to raise as her son.

Temujin's message was loud and clear. Those who followed him would be treated with kindness and mercy. Those who betrayed him would be killed.

CHAPTER 13

Battle with Gur-Khan

Temujin and Toghril join forces AGAINST JAMUKA.

JAMUKA REFUSED to let Temujin's show of power worry him. In four years, he was ready to challenge his *anda* again.

Jamuka called his followers to a meeting. The Merkid leaders came. The powerful Naiman chiefs were there. So were Temujin's old enemies, the Tayichiud. The leaders renewed their alliance. Then they gave Jamuka the title of *Gur-Khan*, or "khan of all khans."

The act was an insult to both Toghril and Temujin. It was time for another showdown.

The Gur-Khan led his army onto the steppe. Toghril and Temujin led their forces to meet them. The two sides then put on a show. They tried to frighten each other into retreat. Warriors sacrificed animals to their gods. Shaman priests climbed onto high rocks. They beat their drums. They used magical jada stones to try to change the weather.

According to *The Secret History*, Temujin's shamans did their job well. The night before the battle, great claps of thunder rang out. The sky opened up and rain poured down. Jamuka's warriors were either frightened or blocked by mud. They began to retreat with Toghril's warriors behind them.

Temujin split from Toghril's forces to chase the Tayichiud. The two armies rode hard toward the Onon River. After they crossed the river, the Tayichiud turned to fight. Archers shot arrows from horseback. Riders swung at each other with long poles. All day, the

TEMUJIN'S HORSEMEN CHASED down the Tayichiud. Temujin then had most of the leaders killed.

battle went back and forth. Neither side seemed to gain an advantage. Near dusk, an arrow opened a wound on Temujin's neck. He left the battlefield. Darkness fell and the two sides settled in for the night.

In Temujin's camp, the khan lay bleeding. The arrow may have been tipped with poison. Temujin's former servant, Jelme, came to his side. For hours, Jelme sucked blood from the wound.

Finally, Temujin woke up. When he complained of thirst, Jelme risked his life to sneak into the Tayichiud camp. He stole some yogurt to bring back to Temujin. "You have saved my life," Temujin told him. "I will never forget the services you have rendered."

By morning, most of the enemy had decided the battle couldn't be won. They fled into the forest. Temujin and his men chased down the Tayichiud warriors. While Temujin rode, he heard a woman's voice calling his name. It had been 25 years since Temujin was a prisoner of the Tayichiud. But he still remembered the family that had helped him escape. The woman calling him was the daughter of the old man.

Temujin had the Tayichiud leaders killed. But he freed the servant woman's family and took them into his tribe. That night, they camped near the tent of the great Mongol leader.

CHAPTER 14

The New Order

Temujin gets rid of the Tatars and begins to BUILD AN EMPIRE.

TEMUJIN CAME BACK TO CAMP after defeating the Tayichiud. He learned that Jamuka had slipped away from Toghril. Still, he was determined to bring the entire steppe under his leadership. To do that, he needed total control over his own warriors.

Temujin gave a new set of orders that must have shocked the clan leaders. In war, warriors were not to stop fighting until the enemy was defeated. Then, they would collect the loot in an orderly way. Everything must be delivered to Temujin and his close advisors.

The khan would decide how to divide up the goods. Anyone who disobeyed the order would be executed.

In 1202, these orders were tested. Temujin went to war against the mighty Tatars. For centuries, the Tatars had done what they wanted on the steppe. They had more warriors, more wealth, and better weapons than the Mongols. Under Temujin, the Mongols had the strength to fight back.

A MONGOL WARRIOR SPEARS A TATAR with his lance. In a few short months, the Mongols nearly wiped out the powerful Tatars.

The newly organized army was a total success. The Mongols swept east toward the enemy. Arrows filled the dry air over the steppe. The Tatars were quickly defeated.

Three clan leaders failed to follow Temujin's new orders. In a rare show of mercy, Temujin let them live. But he took every last bit of their loot.

Temujin now had a new problem. The Tatars were a tribe of many thousands of people. Normally, the Mongols would return home with their loot. They would take some of the Tatars as slaves. The rest would be left to grow in strength. In a few years, they would be fighting again.

Temujin had a different goal. He wanted to wipe out old tribal divisions. To do that, he needed to turn the Tatars into Mongols.

Temujin's followers met to discuss the problem. Together, the clan leaders decided the fate of the Tatars. They chose to kill every male taller than the axle of a cart. Everyone else would become part of the tribe. Temujin himself took two Tatar women. They joined Borte as wives of the khan.

In a matter of months, the most powerful tribe on the steppe disappeared.

Temujin now ruled over many thousands of people. He needed to make sure they all stayed loyal to him, not to local tribal leaders. He reorganized his army into units of ten. The soldiers in each unit would fight as brothers, no matter what clan they belonged to. Ten units joined together to make a company of a hundred warriors. Ten companies formed a division of a thousand.

Temujin named commanders for each company. Tribal leaders were not his first choice. He wanted military men who were talented and loyal. Many of the commanders he chose came from the lower classes. They were shepherds and carpenters. Jelme, the son of a blacksmith, was a top commander.

Another commander came from the hated Tayichiud clan. He had killed Temujin's horse in battle. After the battle, the man came to Temujin to ask forgiveness.

Temujin was impressed with his honesty. He named the warrior Jebe, or arrow. "Such a man is worthy of being a companion," Temujin said.

The new system turned the Mongol army into a fighting machine. Temujin gave orders to just a few commanders. They spread the word to the others. It was quick and simple.

The system required another important invention. The Mongols had no written language. Orders had to be given to a messenger. The messenger then rode as fast as possible. He repeated the message to the commander it was meant for.

To speed the process, Temujin formed a pony express. He created a series of stations across the steppe. Each station had fresh horses and fresh messengers. Riders stopped at the stations to pass their message on. The messages traveled as fast as a rested horse could run.

Temujin had his forces in order. He was ready for the final showdown with Jamuka.

But first, he would have to deal with Toghril.

JEBE BECAME A GREAT MONGOL WARRIOR. Here, Jebe (center) leads a charge, sword raised, with Genghis Khan close behind.

CHAPTER 15

Betrayal

TEMUJIN GOES TO WAR with his old ally, Toghril.

AFTER DEFEATING THE TATARS, Temujin sent a message to Toghril. He wanted his son Jochi to marry Toghril's daughter. In return, he would send his own daughter to marry one of Toghril's sons.

It was a smart move for Temujin. For years, Toghril had been the most powerful leader on the steppe. Now, he was an old man. When he died, someone would take his place. And there were two obvious choices: Temujin and Jamuka. By accepting the marriage proposals, Toghril would signal his choice. Temujin would lead the Kerait after the old man's death.

At first Toghril rejected the offer. Then he seemed to change his mind. He invited Temujin to a wedding ceremony.

Temujin set out with a few companions. Along the way, a shepherd warned him that Toghril's offer was a trap. Toghril, the shepherd said, planned to murder Temujin and his family.

Temujin quickly turned around. Toghril's army followed close behind. Taken by surprise, Temujin fled with just a small group of followers. The group staggered east, running low on food. Finally Toghril's army gave up the chase. Temujin's ragged group arrived on the shores of Lake Baljuna. There they set up camp.

Suddenly, Temujin's luck had changed. His followers were scattered. Boorchu and other close friends were lost. The leader of the Mongols was trapped in exile, many miles from his homeland.

Temujin had reached a turning point. He had

brought together many clans. But he was weak and separated from them all. The clan leaders could easily give up on him. They could give their support to Jamuka or Toghril.

But right at this moment, Temujin's luck began to change again. Boorchu showed up, alive and well. So did Temujin's son Ogodei. Temujin sent messages across the steppe. He asked his followers to join him. One by one, they arrived.

TEMUJIN HAD FOUR SONS (above). Only Ogodei seems to have been with him at Baljuna Lake.

Nineteen leaders gathered around Temujin. They came from different clans and tribes. They worshipped different gods. Some were Christian. Some were Buddhist. Others, like Temujin, prayed to the gods of nature.

One night, Temujin lifted a cup of muddy water from the lake. He told the leaders he was ready for the final battle on the steppe. He asked for their support. He promised to share the fruits of battle with his allies. "If I break my word," he said, "may I become as the waters of the Baljuna."

The men drank. Then they prepared for war.

Temujin led his armies west across the steppe. They gathered strength as they rode. More and more clans joined the march.

Temujin prepared a surprise attack on the Kerait. First he tricked Toghril into laying down his defenses. He sent a message saying he was ready to forget about the past. He wanted to rejoin Toghril.

Toghril was pleased. He sent his own messenger back to Temujin to accept the offer. But Temujin's army was already on its way. His soldiers captured the messenger and killed him. They rode through the night to meet the Kerait.

The Mongol army swept into the Kerait camp during a feast. The Kerait were surprised, but they fought fiercely. The battle raged for three days.

Finally, the Kerait surrendered. Toghril was killed trying to escape. He had been like a father to Temujin. But he betrayed his adopted son. And now he was dead.

That left only Temujin's blood brother, Jamuka.

CHAPTER 16

Death of a Brother

Jamuka fights TO THE END.

IN TWO YEARS, TEMUJIN HAD DEFEATED two of the big tribal powers on the steppe: the Tatars and the Kerait. But he was still outnumbered. The Naiman lay to the west with an army of thousands. They had the support of the Merkid and other small tribes. The Naiman also had Jamuka with them.

In 1204, Temujin was ready to do battle. He led his army west from the sacred mountain Burkhan Khaldun. They rode 300 miles across the steppe. The Naiman forces rode to meet them.

In his final test on the steppe, Temujin showed his skill as a commander. The Naiman army filled the battlefield. It was far larger than Temujin's forces. So Temujin had his front line play a trick. Each soldier lit five fires at night. The Naiman warriors saw a sea of flickering light. Temujin's army looked much greater than it was.

GATHERING FOR WAR: Eight hundred years after the death of Genghis Khan, Mongolian horsemen ride into battle for a 2003 movie about his life.

As the fighting started, Temujin launched a series of small hit-and-run attacks. He called it the Moving Bush Formation. Units of ten sneaked up on the Naimans before dawn. They shot their arrows from different directions. Then they ran, leaving the enemy confused.

Temujin followed with the Lake Formation. Long lines of men advanced in waves. One after another, the lines shot their arrows.

To meet the attacks, the Naiman had to stretch their line of defence. Then Temujin switched to the Chisel Formation. He arranged his men in a triangle, pointed at the front. The attack drove deep into the Naiman lines.

Finally, the Naiman army fled. Temujin pushed them to the foothills of the Altai Mountains. The Naiman tried to get away by climbing down steep cliffs. In the darkness, hundreds fell to their death.

The war for control of the Mongols was over.

Jamuka escaped into the mountains. Most of his followers deserted him. Only a few friends stayed. The small band wandered for another year. Without a tribe, they survived by hunting wild animals. Finally, Jamuka's friends betrayed him. They seized their leader and brought him to Temujin.

Temujin's response was typical. He hated disloyalty of any kind. He punished people who betrayed their leaders—even when those leaders were his enemies. This time was no different. Temujin gathered the traitors. He had them executed in front of Jamuka.

Then he turned to a painful task. Jamuka had been his closest friend as a child. They were blood brothers. What would Temujin do with him now?

According to *The Secret History*, Temujin asked Jamuka to be his ally once again. Jamuka answered that he could not be a good friend. Temujin would never trust him. He wanted only to be killed quickly. He asked Temujin to bury him on high ground. From there, his spirit would watch over Temujin forever.

Temujin gave the order. Jamuka was killed. According to Mongol legend, Temujin found a gold sash he had given Jamuka. He had his old friend buried with the gift.

One by one, Temujin had gotten rid of his rivals. More than 30 years before, his brother Begter had been the first to go. His blood brother Jamuka now became the latest. At the age of 43, Temujin had won. He had created a nation out of a group of warring nomadic tribes. He ruled about one million people. His land stretched across an area the size of Western Europe. He stood alone as ruler of all the Mongols.

Genghis Khan in Pictures

ONE ARTIST'S VIEW

No one knows exactly what Genghis Khan looked like. During his lifetime he never let anyone draw his portrait. This woodcut was created by an artist in China.

BORN IN A YURT

The Mongolian Steppe looks much the same today as it did in the 12th century. Genghis Khan grew up in yurts like these. His family struggled to stay alive on the dry plains. They moved with the seasons to find good hunting or pasture land.

HELD CAPTIVE

When Temujin was a teen, Tayichiud warriors took him prisoner. They locked him in a yoke like this one.

TEMUJIN'S CHILD BRIDE

When Temujin was just nine years old, his father, Yesugei, set up his marriage to a girl named Borte. On the way home, Yesugei was killed. Temujin didn't see Borte for seven years. At 16, he returned to claim her as his bride.

A POWERFUL ALLY

Temujin's first important ally was Toghril, the leader of the Kerait. Temujin met with him in Toghril's golden yurt, which may have looked like the ones above.

THE MONGOLIAN HORDES

Mongol warriors were known for their skills on horseback. The horsemen carried everything they needed on their backs. If they grew desperate with hunger, they were known to slit a horse's vein and drink the blood.

ON THE WARPATH

For 20 years, Genghis Khan did battle with the other tribes of the steppe. Since the Mongols rode without foot soldiers, they moved faster than any army the world had seen.

RULER OF ALL THE MONGOLS

By 1206, Temujin had conquered all the tribes of the steppe. He called the leaders of the tribes together near the place where he was born. He had himself declared Genghis Khan, ruler of all the Mongols.

INVASION INTO CHINA

In 1211, Genghis Khan led his warriors against the Jurched in northern China. The Mongols killed thousands during a great battle in the mountains.

RELIGIOUS TOLERANCE

In 1220, the Mongols moved west, into the Muslim empire of Khwarizm. Genghis Khan often destroyed the cities he conquered. But he allowed people to worship their own gods. This painting shows Genghis Khan (top right) speaking from the stairs of a mosque in the city of Bukhara. He took the city's religious leaders under his protection.

FINDING A SUCCESSOR
In 1219, Genghis Khan (top) wanted to choose a successor. He called his four sons (lined up at right) together. After a fight between Jochi and Chagatai, Genghis Khan chose Ogodei.

A SECRET BURIAL GROUND
Genghis Khan died in 1227. He was buried in great secrecy. No one knows the location of his grave. His capital, Karakorum, however, is the site of an old Buddhist monastery. It's guarded by a stone tortoise and a line of Buddhist statues.

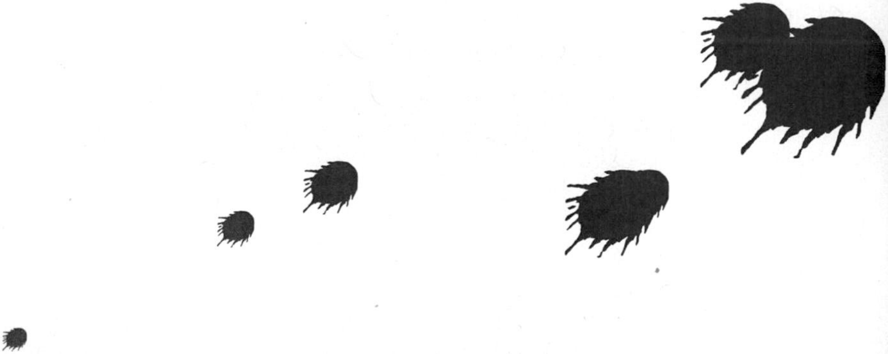

Part 3

Genghis Khan's World War

CHAPTER 17

From Temujin to Genghis Khan

The Khan of all the Mongols takes over and MAKES HIS MARK.

IN 1206, TEMUJIN CALLED all the Mongol leaders together. They met at the source of the Onon River. Temujin was returning to his roots. His family had camped there when the Tayichiud first deserted them. He wanted to remind the Mongols how far he had come.

Beside the Onon, the Mongols named Temujin their leader. They gave him the title *Genghis Khan.*

The name *Genghis* probably comes from a Mongolian word meaning "strong."

The tribes celebrated for days. Thousands of followers put up yurts nearby. They raised banners with horsetails attached. They feasted on meat from sheep and goats grazing outside the camp. Shamans beat their drums and asked the sky god to protect the great khan. Young men competed in wrestling and archery.

Meanwhile, Genghis Khan set down the rules of his nation. For many centuries, the Mongol tribes had argued and fought with each other. Now they had to act and fight as one. Bringing them together was no easy task.

Genghis Khan gave positions of great power to his loyal friends. Boorchu commanded 10,000 warriors. Jebe won another command post. Eventually he would lead 20,000 men into battle. Genghis Khan also gave command posts to his sons, Jochi, Chagatai, Ogodei, and Tolui.

Next, he started a military draft. All men between 15 and 70 had to serve in the army. Most soldiers were separated from their tribal leaders. From now on, they would obey only their military commander. The commanders also had power over their soldiers' families.

Finally, he created a system of laws. To record the laws, he gave the Mongols a written language. It came from a Turkish tribe called the Uighur.

Genghis Khan's new scribes were put to work right away. Their first job was the book of Great Laws or *Yasa*. With the *Yasa*, Genghis Khan tried to bring order to the steppe. He banned the kidnapping of women. He made it a crime to enslave a Mongol. Stealing was also illegal. The punishment for thieves was death.

Some of the laws in the *Yasa* were harsh. But Genghis Khan also let many of the tribes keep their local customs. He insisted on freedom of religion. Muslims, Christians, and Buddhists could worship as they pleased. Genghis Khan wanted them all to feel welcome under his rule.

Some of the harshest laws were reserved for the army. In battle, there was no room for disobedience. Death was the punishment for soldiers who kept loot for themselves. Messengers who got drunk on duty could also be executed.

Under the new rules, the Mongol army became a force to be feared. It was more powerful than any yet seen on earth. The question was, where would it turn next?

ON THE THRONE AT LAST: Near the source of the Onon River, Temujin has himself proclaimed Genghis Khan.

Chapter 18

Ready for War

The Mongol army is ON THE MOVE.

GENGHIS KHAN HAD WON THE TRUST of a million people. But in one way he was no different from other rulers on the steppe. His power as khan came with expectations. The Mongols looked to Genghis Khan to make them rich.

There was just one problem. The flow of looted goods had been cut off. The nomadic tribes were all part of the same nation now. The *Yasa* put a stop to the age-old tradition of raiding your neighbor.

Genghis Khan needed a new supply of wealth.

And he had to go to war to get it. In 1210, he decided on his target.

That year, the Golden Khan of the wealthy Jurched died. His son became the new Jurched leader. For years, the Jurched had considered themselves superior to the nomadic tribes. Toghril had promised his loyalty to the Golden Khan. The new Golden Khan wanted the same promise from Genghis Khan.

He sent an ambassador to meet with the Mongol leader. The two men met on the steppe. The Jurched ambassador demanded Genghis Khan's loyalty. He may have expected the Mongol leader to kneel. Perhaps he expected a gift. Instead, Genghis Khan turned toward the Jurched homeland and spat on the dusty ground. He shouted insults in the Golden Khan's direction. Then he rode off to the north.

War had been declared.

In the spring of 1211, the Mongols prepared for battle. Genghis Khan raised an army of about 65,000 horsemen. They knew they were outnumbered. The

Jurched had at least that many horsemen. They were supported by 85,000 foot soldiers. And the Jurched probably had unlimited replacements. Their empire contained 50 million people in all.

Despite the difference in numbers, the Mongols had an important advantage. They moved faster than any army on earth. They had no foot soldiers. And they never had to wait for supply wagons. Each soldier carried his own supplies.

According to the Italian traveler Marco Polo, the Mongols could ride for ten days without stopping to cook food. They hunted and looted when their supplies ran low. If they ran out of water, they cut open a horse's vein and drank the blood.

In May of 1211, the Mongol army assembled. They divided into divisions of a thousand. Then they set off across the steppe, rumbling south toward the empire of the Jurched.

The Fiercest Warriors on Earth

GENGHIS KHAN'S MONGOL WARRIORS WERE FIERCE. They were also prepared. Each man carried everything he needed. He had a bow and arrows. He carried spare clothing, a knife, and a hatchet. He had rope and two canteens. One canteen contained water. In the other he mixed water with dried milk.

Each soldier also carried dried meat and cheese. The entire army ate while it rode. When the soldiers had fresh meat, they carried it under their saddles to soften it for eating.

THIS IMAGE OF A MONGOL WARRIOR was created in the 1200s. It shows the warrior's bow, lance, and saber.

CHAPTER 19

Conquest of the Jurched

THE MONGOLS FACE the walled cities of northern China.

WITH GREAT SPEED, Jebe led the Mongols across the burning Gobi desert. In the east, they moved quickly through the land known today as Manchuria. In the mountains to the west, they ran into the ancient forerunner of the Great Wall of China.

In the east, their first task was to convince the people of the countryside to revolt. About 100 years earlier the Jurched had taken northern China from a tribe called the Khitan. In 1212, along the eastern front, Genghis Khan announced his arrival to the Khitan. He was here to free them from Jurched rule, he said. If they joined the Mongol nation, they would be treated kindly.

All throughout the war, Khitan leaders joined up with Genghis Khan. In the spring of 1212, a Khitan leader put together an army of 100,000 men. He agreed to fight alongside the Mongols.

By the fall of 1213, the entire Mongol army had broken through the walls in the mountains. As they marched through northern China, they welcomed Khitan rebels.

But the Mongols were ruthless to those who refused to join them. They destroyed farmland as they rode. Terrified farmers fled to the walled cities of the Jurched. More than a million people left their homes by the end of the war. Food supplies ran low. People in the cities starved. Reports leaked out that the Jurched were eating human flesh to survive.

Often, the Mongols put captives to work. When they came to a village, each invading soldier took ten prisoners. The prisoners fed the Mongol horses. They brought water for the soldiers. They hauled dirt to fill in the moats that protected the cities.

The lives of these prisoners meant little to the Mongol soldiers. During dangerous attacks, they were often shoved to the front. The Mongols used them as human shields. As the prisoners died, their bodies filled the moats along with the dirt they had carried.

As the war dragged on, Genghis Khan learned urban warfare. Unlike the Mongols, the Jurched lived in cities protected by walls made of wood and stone. The Mongols built dams on nearby rivers to flood the cities. They also copied the high-tech weapons used by the Jurched. The most important of these was the catapult. These huge machines flung stones or burning oil at city walls.

The Mongols also learned to build ballistas. These machines worked like enormous archer's bows. They shot powerful arrows that could break through buildings or walls. Eventually, the Mongols discovered the Chinese firelance. The firelance was a bamboo tube stuffed with gunpowder. It worked like a flamethrower. In about 30 years, it would evolve into the world's first gun.

Wherever they could, the Mongols found Jurched men who were trained to build these machines. They treated these engineers well if they would work for the Mongols. Most people knew what would happen if they refused. Few were foolish enough to say no.

With help from their new weapons, Mongol soldiers pushed their way through Jurched land. For three years, they destroyed the countryside. They captured cities. They picked up allies as they rode.

Finally Genghis Khan arrived at Zhongdu. A sea of horsemen surrounded the Jurched capital. Inside, the Golden Khan was trapped.

The Jurched ruler met with Mongol messengers and agreed to a deal. He promised his loyalty to Genghis Khan. Then he gave the Mongols what they wanted. He produced huge amounts of silk, gold, and silver. To Genghis Khan himself, he gave a princess, 1,000 slaves, and 3,000 horses. The Golden Khan also promised to pay a tax. He would send goods north to the Mongols every year.

Genghis Khan was satisfied. He had access to Jurched riches. He had no desire to control the land. The Khitan would have their nation back. The Golden Khan would

AT ZHONGDU, Genghis Khan used the Jurched's own war machines to batter the walls of their capital city.

keep a small part of his empire. Rulers of both lands would recognize the Mongols as their lords.

Genghis Khan left some soldiers behind to guard Zhongdu. The rest of the Mongol army headed home.

The Jurched, however, ignored their promise. The Golden Khan and his staff fled their capital. To Genghis Khan, this was an act of rebellion. He sent his horsemen racing back to Zhongdu. The city fell quickly. A month of looting followed. Fires raged. Thousands of people were massacred. One visitor said the bones piled outside the city looked like a white hill.

Now, the Mongols were there to stay. Genghis Khan had conquered a vast part of northern China.

The Mongol leader left his trusted commander, Mukali, to rule the entire area. He placed an army of 60,000 men under Mukali's control. The rest of the warriors returned home. On their way, they trampled farmland and tore up fences. Much of the Jurched empire became pasture land for Mongol herds.

A Great Wall

THE GREAT WALL OF CHINA IS THE LARGEST structure ever built by humans. And it wouldn't exist without the Mongols.

When Genghis Khan invaded China, he ran into a wall of earth and stones just south of the Gobi desert. Sections of it had been there for 1,200 years. The Mongols broke through and began their conquest of China. Starting in 1279, Mongol emperors ruled all of China for nearly 100 years.

In 1449, the Mongols attacked again. The Ming rulers of China began rebuilding the wall. Over the next 200 years, tens of thousands of workers built one of the seven wonders of the world out of bricks and stone. By 1644, the wall stretched for 3,948 miles.

THE GREAT WALL that stands today was built in the 1400s to keep the descendants of Genghis Khan out of China.

CHAPTER 20

Family Feud

WHO WILL TAKE OVER when Genghis Khan is gone?

IN THE SPRING OF 1215, the Mongols were treated to an incredible sight. Long lines of ox carts, camels, and horses returned from northern China. Each cart brought a new load of glimmering loot taken from the Jurched. Workmen unloaded piles of silk in bright colors. They unpacked metal armor, pots, and knives. They discovered unusual games and new medicines.

Genghis Khan had succeeded beyond anyone's dreams. And the new wealth changed the way the Mongols lived. Buildings were constructed to store the loot. The compound became known as the Yellow Palace. Many people now had wood furniture in their yurts. They got rid of their rawhide cord and used silk instead. Horsemen put their feet in metal stirrups. Warriors fought with iron weapons.

The Mongols also brought back craftsmen to make new goods. Tailors, blacksmiths, and jewelers came with them as prisoners. Scribes taught writing to the Mongols. Doctors made medicines for them. Musicians and jugglers entertained them.

It was a new world on the steppe. And Genghis Khan spent several years keeping that world in order. He handed out the loot according to strict rules. He put down rebellions on the steppe. He tried to open trade with the Muslims to the west.

By 1219 the great khan was 57 years old. A visitor described him as a tall, strong man with "great energy." His eyes were lively like a cat's. Still, he was showing signs of age. The hair on his face had turned snow white. After all, in his day, few people lived to be 60.

At 57, Genghis Khan was an old man.

It was time for the old man to settle an important question. Who would take over the empire after he died?

Genghis Khan called his four sons to a meeting. Jochi, Chagatai, Ogodei and Tolui appeared before their father. Jochi was the oldest. Genghis Khan made it clear that he stood first in line to become khan.

Chagatai, the next oldest, became furious. Jochi didn't even share their father's blood, he said. He was the son of a Merkid kidnapper. Chagatai refused to serve under him.

Jochi exploded in anger. The two brothers lunged at each other. Genghis Khan sat in silence while his sons fought.

When the fight was broken up, the father spoke. Chagatai had not just insulted Jochi, Genghis Khan said. Chagatai had insulted his own mother. Genghis Khan reminded his sons how hard he had worked to build an empire. He did not want to see it ruined by a family argument.

After listening to his father, Chagatai suggested a compromise. Ogodei should be khan, he said. Ogodei wasn't perfect. He was unpredictable at times. He drank too much. But he was generous and good-hearted. Besides, he was probably the only choice. Tolui had great skills in battle. But he was young and showed signs of cruelty. Jochi and Chagatai had to be ruled out. There would be civil war if either one became khan.

Finally, everyone agreed. The sons knelt before their father. After Genghis Khan's death, Ogodei would rule the Mongols. Genghis Khan then gave each son a part of the empire. He made sure Jochi and Chagatai were separated by many miles.

With the question settled, Genghis Khan turned his attention to the west. A sultan had challenged the Mongols. It was time to go to war again.

OGODEI, one of Genghis Khan's four sons, became Khan of the Mongols after his father's death. He held the position for 12 years.

CHAPTER 21

Central Asia Is Next

The Mongols invade A MUSLIM EMPIRE.

TO THE WEST OF THE MONGOLS lay a huge Muslim empire called Khwarizm. It stretched 1,500 miles from east to west. The empire began in the mountains of modern Afghanistan. It ended at the Black Sea. It went from the Aral Sea in the north to the Persian Gulf in the south. All of it was ruled by Muhammad II, sultan of Khwarizm.

The Mongols were hungry for the goods produced

in Khwarizm. Muslim craftsmen knew the secrets of steel. They made weapons out of the shiny and powerful metal. Experts understood how to make glass. Tailors sewed beautiful clothes out of cotton.

Genghis Khan wanted access to the riches of Khwarizm. When he returned from China, he sent a messenger to the sultan. "I am master of the eastern lands," he said. "You are master of the western lands." He proposed a treaty between the two rulers. Merchants would be allowed to come and go in peace.

The sultan agreed reluctantly to the treaty. He considered the Mongols to be savages. But he knew that they had conquered the Jurched. He wasn't prepared to go to war against an army that powerful.

In 1218, Genghis Khan sent merchants to Otrar, a city in the far east of the sultan's empire. Their carts were loaded with goods to trade. The governor of the city sent word to the sultan. The traders had come to spy on the empire, he said. With the sultan's support, the governor had the traders murdered.

GENGHIS KHAN SPOKE to the people of Bukhara in their Muslim mosque. As a rule, Genghis Khan (top right) had respect for other religions.

Once again, an ally had betrayed Genghis Khan. The great khan responded quickly and brutally. He set out with a force of about 100,000. In the fall of 1219, Mongol horsemen surrounded Otrar. The siege took five months, but the city finally fell. About 20,000 defenders were killed. Mongol warriors captured the governor and executed him.

Genghis Khan and Tolui had already moved on to the west. They arrived with a large force outside Bukhara in February. Thousands of troops fled when they heard the horsemen. The rest of the city surrendered a day later.

The Mongols gave the residents the usual treatment. Soldiers were killed immediately. Other men were rounded up. They would be used as shields during the next battle. People with skills were separated from the rest. Doctors and teachers were important to the Mongols. So were metal workers, weapon makers, and other craftsmen. Genghis Khan offered these people jobs. If they accepted, the Mongols treated them well.

In March, Genghis Khan arrived at Samarkand, the sultan's capital. It was surrounded by high walls. More than 100,000 soldiers defended it. Yet it fell within ten days.

The Mongols moved on to Tirmiz and other cities. The Khwarizm Empire was crumbling. Muhammad II fled to an island in the Caspian Sea. He died there in 1221. His son, Jalal-ad-Din, escaped to India. He fought on for another decade. But Khwarizm had fallen to Genghis Khan.

During the war, the Mongols destroyed dozens of cities. They changed trade routes completely. They turned thousands of acres of farmland into pasture. The number of people they killed may have reached the millions.

The great Mongol khan now ruled an empire 3,000 miles wide. In his own words, his land stretched from the rising sun to the setting sun. And yet, there was one thing he still wanted desperately. He wished to live forever.

CHAPTER 22

The Last Campaign

Nearing the end, Genghis Khan SETTLES ONE LAST SCORE.

IN 1222, GENGHIS KHAN CAMPED in the mountains of the land known today as Afghanistan. He waited impatiently for a visitor. During the Jurched war, he had heard of a Chinese holy man named Changchun. Supposedly, Changchun had found the secret to long life. According to legend, he had reached the age of 300. Genghis Khan sent for him, and the holy man was on his way.

Changchun arrived at the Mongol camp. As it turned out, he was not a day over 75. He told Genghis

Khan that the stories were false. He could not keep anyone from dying. He could only give them medicines to fight disease.

Despite his disappointment, Genghis Khan liked the holy man. They met often during the next few months. Changchun advised Genghis Khan to live a quieter life. He told him to be kind to his people. He suggested he give up hunting. Genghis Khan had Changchun's words written down. He asked the holy man to pray for him.

By 1226, however, Genghis Khan was ill. And he was not in the mood to live quietly. To the south, the Tangut had rebelled against the Mongols. Genghis Khan led his troops into battle one final time.

Genghis Khan could feel death coming on. He called Ogodei and Tolui to his side. Chagatai was at home. Jochi had died two years earlier. After the meeting in 1219, Jochi had never spoken to his father again. Genghis Khan saw him as a threat. There were rumors that the great khan killed his own son.

Now, Ogodei and Tolui gathered around their father. Genghis Khan told his sons to work together. He told them an old story about a many-headed snake. The snake was crushed by a cart because it could not decide which way to go. Do not be like the many-headed snake, Genghis Khan told his sons. He insisted that they rule with only one head. Then he made them sign a paper naming Ogodei as khan.

With Genghis Khan dying, the Mongols wanted

ON HIS DEATHBED, Genghis Khan urged his sons to stick together after he was gone.

to call off the attack. They sent a message of peace to the Tangut king. His reply was insulting. According to *The Secret History*, Genghis Khan was "on fire with fever." But he was determined to finish the war. In August 1227, the Mongols forced the Tangut king to surrender.

Just a few days earlier, Genghis Khan had died.

The Mongol army took out their anger on the Tangut people. Everyone in the capital city was killed.

The army then placed Genghis Khan's body in a cart. They set off for the Mongol homeland. Genghis Khan had ordered that his death be kept secret. Legend has it that everyone who saw the funeral procession was killed.

When the caravan arrived home, Genghis Khan was buried. To this day, no one knows where. Most people think he was returned to the place he loved most: the mountain of Burkhan Khaldun.

Wicked?

Genghis Khan's sons and grandsons followed him as khan. For fifty years, the empire expanded. By 1279, it was bigger than any empire ever seen on earth. The Mongol khan ruled 20 million square miles and 100 million people. Today, that land is home to half the people in the world.

No one conquers more than half the world without relying on violence. But was Genghis Khan really a monster?

Some people are convinced that he was. He ordered the deaths of hundreds of thousands of people, perhaps millions. Many enemy soldiers were executed after they had surrendered. Many more victims weren't even soldiers.

Genghis Khan also destroyed dozens of cities. He ruined farmland and turned farmers into homeless wanderers. He destroyed the trade routes of Central

Asia. Southern Russia was turned into a wasteland by his troops. From East Asia to Eastern Europe, people had nightmares about Genghis Khan. They feared being trampled by Mongol horsemen.

To some people, however, Genghis Khan is a hero. In Mongolia, he is considered a great leader. His conquests are shown in paintings. His face appears on postage stamps. He did, after all, stop centuries of warfare between the Mongol tribes. He brought goods home from the far corners of the earth. He made the Mongols rich.

Supporters argue that he had many admirable qualities. He didn't favor the rich and powerful. Common people could rise to great heights in his empire. They simply needed to show talent and loyalty. People of all faiths were treated equally, as well. Christians, Buddhists, and Muslims worshipped freely in the Mongol empire. Genghis Khan was generous to his followers. He gave most of his captured wealth away while he himself lived simply. In war, he was ruthless, but he never used torture. When his warriors killed, they did it quickly.

Yet, there is no question that Genghis Khan was ruthless. When people betrayed him, second chances were rare. Insults were not forgotten. Revenge was the law of the steppe and Genghis Khan enforced it with great violence. In war, he had only one goal—to defeat the enemy completely. No act was too terrible if it brought him closer to that goal. Use innocent farmers as human shields? Of course, he would say—if it helps win the war. His central rule on the battlefield was this: Reward the people who give in, and kill those who resist.

You could say that there were two sides to Genghis Khan's personality. One was loyal, generous, and open-minded. The other was vengeful, bloodthirsty, and secretive.

Does one side or the other represent the "real" Genghis Khan? That's up to you to decide.

Timeline of Terror

1162

1162: Temujin, who would become Genghis Khan, is born.

1171: Temujin's father, Yesugei, is poisoned.

1173: Jamuka and Temujin become blood brothers.

1175: Temujin and his brother, Khasar, kill their half brother, Begter.

1178: Temujin claims his bride, Borte. He makes an alliance with Toghril, leader of the Kerait.

1179: Temujin, Jamuka, and Toghril attack the Merkid.

1181: Jamuka and Temujin go their separate ways.

1189: Temujin claims the title of khan.

1190: Jamuka and Temujin fight their first battle with each other. Jamuka takes brutal revenge on Temujin's followers.

1195: Temujin joins Toghril and the Jurched in fighting the Tatars.

1197: Temujin brutally gets rid of leaders of the Jurkin clan.

1201: Temujin and Toghril go to war against Jamuka, the Merkid, the Naiman, and the Tayichiud. Temujin defeats the Tayichiud.

1202: Temujin conquers the Tatars and reorganizes his army.

1203: Temujin defeats his old ally, Toghril.

1204: Temujin finally defeats Jamuka and his Naiman allies. Jamuka is executed.

1206: Temujin becomes Genghis Khan, ruler of the united Mongols.

1211: Genghis Khan declares war against the Jurched and the Golden Khan.

1215: Genghis Khan's forces conquer Zhongdu, the Jurched capital.

1219: Genghis Khan chooses his successor—his son Ogodei. The Mongols begin their conquest of the empire of Khwarizm.

1227: Genghis Khan dies; the Tangut are defeated.

1227

Until about 1200, it's hard to know exactly when the events in Genghis Khan's life happened. Many of these dates are approximations.

Glossary

alliance (uh-LYE-uhnss) ***noun*** an agreement to work together

ally (AL-eye) ***noun*** a person or country that gives support to another

andas (AHN-duhs) ***noun*** in Mongol culture, friends who proved the closeness of their bond by drinking each other's blood

archer (AR-chur) ***noun*** a person who uses a bow and arrow

ballista (buh-LIS-tuh) ***noun*** a weapon that worked like a giant crossbow; it shot arrows that could break through the walls of buildings

blacksmith (BLAK-smith) ***noun*** someone who makes and fits horseshoes and fixes things made of iron

Buddhist (BOO-dist) ***noun*** a person who practices Buddhism, a religion based on the teachings of Buddha and practiced mainly in eastern and central Asia

caravan (KA-ruh-van) ***noun*** a group of people traveling together

catapult (KAT-uh-puhlt) ***noun*** a weapon, similar to a large slingshot, used for firing rocks over castle walls

civilized (SIV-i-lized) ***adjective*** highly developed and organized

clan (KLAN) ***noun*** an extended family group

descendant (di-SEND-uhnt) ***noun*** a person's child, grandchild, or other such relative on into the future

empire (EM-pire) ***noun*** a group of countries or regions that have the same ruler

exile (EG-zile) ***noun*** a situation in which one is forced to stay away from one's homeland

firelance (FIRE lanss) ***noun*** a spear-like weapon with a tube containing gunpowder

Genghis Khan (GEN-giss CON) ***noun*** Mongol words meaning "universal ruler"; Mongol leaders gave Temujin this title in 1206

goblet (GOB-lit) ***noun*** a tall drinking container with a stem and base

khan (KON) ***noun*** a Mongol word meaning ruler or leader

Muslim (MUHZ-luhm) ***noun*** someone who follows the religion of Islam, a religion based on the teachings of Muhammad

nomadic (noh-MAD-ik) ***adjective*** wandering from place to place

rawhide (RAW-hide) ***noun*** the skin of cattle or other animals before it has been soaked and made into leather

ruthless (ROOTH-liss) ***adjective*** cruel and without pity

sable (SAY-buhl) ***noun*** a small animal that looks like a weasel; its soft brown fur is very valuable

sacred (SAY-krid) ***adjective*** holy, deserving great respect

scribe (SKRIBE) ***noun*** a person who copies documents by hand

shaman (SHAH-muhn) ***noun*** a person who communicates with the spirit world to help tell the future, control events, or cure the sick

status (STAT-uhss) ***noun*** a person's rank or position in a group

steppe (STEP) ***noun*** treeless plains found in Asia

sultan (SUHLT-uhn) ***noun*** an emperor or ruler of some Muslim countries

tribe (TRIBE) ***noun*** a group of people who share the same ancestors and customs

Yasa (YAH-suh) ***noun*** the code of law created by Genghis Khan

yoke (YOKE) ***noun*** a wooden frame placed around a person's neck to hold him or her prisoner

yurt (YERT) ***noun*** a circular tent made of felt stretched over a light, portable frame of branches

FIND OUT MORE

Here are some books and Web sites with more information about Genghis Khan and his times.

BOOKS

Greenblatt, Miriam. **Genghis Khan and the Mongol Empire (Rulers and Their Times).** New York: Benchmark Books, 2002. (80 pages) *The story of Genghis Khan's life is blended with descriptions of the everyday lives of the Mongol people.*

Lassieur, Allison. **Mongolia (Enchantment of the World: Second Series).** New York: Children's Press, 2007. (144 pages) *Information on the history, people, and geography of Mongolia.*

Rice, Earle Jr. **Empire in the East, The Story of Genghis Khan.** Greensboro, NC: Morgan Reynolds Publishing, 2005. (160 pages) *A beautifully illustrated biography of Genghis Khan.*

Streissguth, Thomas. **Genghis Khan's Mongol Empire (Lost Civilizations).** Farmington Hills, MI: Lucent Books, 2006. (112 pages) *Read how Genghis Khan transformed the Mongols from a divided and poor society into the most feared people on Earth.*

Taylor, Robert. **Life in Genghis Khan's Mongolia (The Way People Live).** San Diego: Lucent Books, 2001. (96 pages) *See how the Mongol people lived during Genghis Khan's time.*

WEB SITES

http://www.lacma.org/khan/index.htm
This web site was created for "The Legacy of Genghis Khan," a 2003 exhibit at the Los Angeles County Museum of Art.

http://www.loc.gov/rr/frd/
The Library of Congress has a great collection of country studies. Go to the site, select "country studies," then choose Mongolia from the list of countries.

http://www.nationalgeographic.com/genghis/index.html
This site includes interviews by a reporter and photographer who traced Genghis Khan's path.

http://www.pbs.org/wnet/nature/mongolia/
A companion to a PBS television series about the nomads of Mongolia and their special relationship with wild horses.

For Grolier subscribers:
http://go.grolier.com/ searches: Genghis Khan; Mongolia

INDEX

Authors' Note and Bibliography

Genghis Khan is known in history as one of the world's great conquerors. His forces attacked and controlled lands from the Pacific Ocean to Europe. Generally, European writers have depicted him as a bloodthirsty, evil man. Mongolian and Chinese authors see another side of him. He respected loyalty and friendships, was open to all religions, and sought to create an empire for his children. The Mongol empire did not long survive him. His children, for the most part, did not have his deep intelligence, his patience, nor his respectful nature.

As you read this book and think about Genghis Khan, you will have to make up your own mind about him. Was he completely evil, or did he have some redeeming virtues? What would be your judgment?

The following books have been most useful in writing and editing Genghis Khan's story:

Atwood, Christopher, ed. **Encyclopedia of Mongolia and the Mongol Empire.** New York: Facts on File, 2004.

Cleaves, Francis Woodman, trans. and ed., **The Secret History of the Mongols.** Cambridge, MA: Harvard University Press, 1982. (This text is the basis of another rendition of **The Secret History** into English in a more poetic style by Paul Khan, Boston: Heng & Tsui Co., 1998. There is another text in English, edited and annotated by Urgunge Onon, London: Routledge Curfzon, 2001.)

Juvaini, Ata-Malik; Boyle John Andrew; and Morgan, David O., trans. and ed. **The History of the World Conqueror.** Manchester, UK: Manchester University Press, 1997.

Man, John. Genghis Khan, **Life, Death and Resurrection.** London: Bantam Press, 2004.

Ratchnevsky, Paul. **Genghis Khan, His Life and Legacy.** Oxford, UK: Blackwell Publishing, 1991.

Roux, Jean-Paul and Ballas, Toula, trans. **Genghis Khan and the Mongol Empire.** London: Thames & Hudson, 2003.

Weatherford, Jack, **Genghis Khan and the Making of the Modern World.** New York: Crown Publishers, 2004.

We are grateful to Jackie Carter, Shari Joffe, and Elizabeth Ward for their work on this project.

Special thanks to our editor, Tod Olson.

—Enid A. Goldberg and Norman Itkowitz